Police Station

by Sheila Anderson

first step nonfiction

Lerner Publications Company · Minneapolis

There is a police station in my community.

It has police cars.

It has jail cells.

It has computers.

It has dogs.

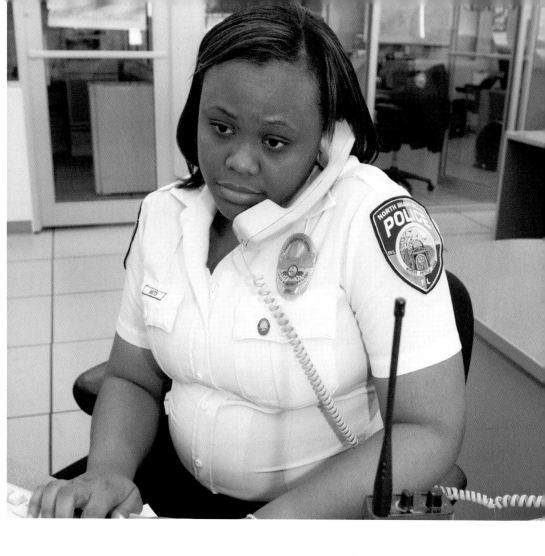

It has police officers.

Have you been to a police station?